THE CAT'S WHISKERS

Written by Val Marshall and Bronwyn Tester
Illustrated by Cam Knuckey

Can you see the black cat?

Midnight black and blue cat.
Silently stalking, rooftop-walking,

Sleek and seeking-rat cat.
Quiet-as-sleeping-bat cat.

Can you see the cat?

Can you catch the ginger cat?

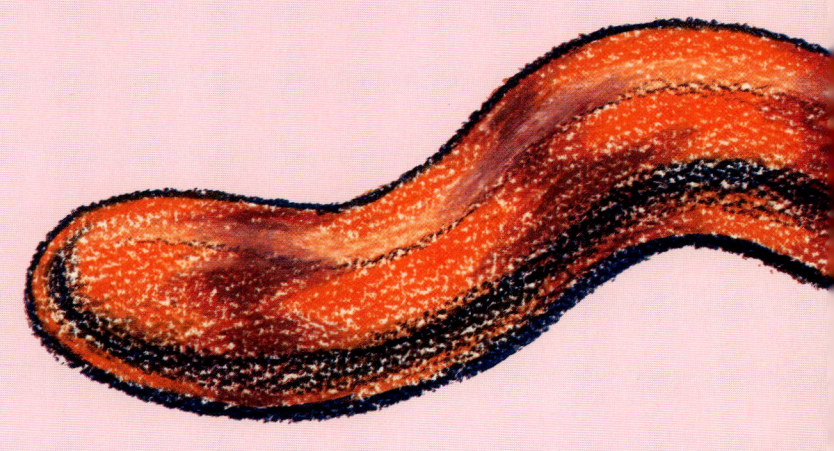

Chasing-through-an-alley cat.
Hackles-rising, dog-despising,

Streaking-up-the-wall cat.
Stealing-food-from-bins cat.

Can you catch the cat?

Can you hear the wild cat?

Screeching, noisy, yowling cat.
Hissing-biting, fiercely fighting,

Fluffed-up tail and stand-up fur,
Stretched-out-on-the-wire cat.

Can you hear the cat?

Can you admire the aristo-cat?

High-heeled, smooth and burnished cat.
Velvet-nosed, ever-composed,

Haughty, proud and pampered cat.
Slinky, whiskered autocrat.

Can you admire the cat?

Can you find the house cat?

Lazy, chase-a-mouse cat.
Sunshine-seeking, cushion-sneaking,

Hiding-in-the-flowerbed cat.
Rubbing-on-your-leg cat.

Can you find the cat?

Can you feel the lap cat?

Comfort-loving, smiling cat.
Softly purring, rarely stirring,

Lazy, have-a-nap cat.
Don't-get-in-a-flap cat.

Can you feel the cat?

But now you must meet my cat.

Brilliant, high-IQ cat.
Clever, read-a-book cat.

Learning-how-to-cook cat.

Singing-on-the-tiles cat.
Full-of-feline-smiles cat.

Snuggles-on-my-bed cat.
Night-turn-out-the-light cat.

Sleeping, quiet,
GOODNIGHT CAT.